an arena, Arles,
ace, A.D. 2nd cent.

Ananda temple, Burma, A.D. 1100

Folding ... C.

Ceremonial ...

Roman
temple

Baalbek, Lebanon, A.D. 2nd cent.

urgical instruments, Greek

early 1st millennium, B.C.

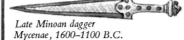

Late Minoan dagger
Mycenae, 1600–1100 B.C.

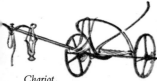

Chariot,
from grave in Thebes, 1350 B.C.

Stonehenge, England, c. 1680 B.C.

Victory of Samothrace,
Greek, 306 B.C.

ABOUT THE COVER

Pompeii, the Forum as it appears today

ACKNOWLEDGMENTS: From C. W. Ceram: *Picture History of Archaeology,* published by Thames and Hudson, Ltd., London: 12 top right, 22, 24 top right and left, 25, 31 bottom left. Art Reference Bureau: 13 bottom right, 27 bottom left, 39 top right. Museum für Volkerkunde, Vienna, photograph by Francis G. Mayer, Art Color Slides, Inc., New York: 16. The Cleveland Museum of Art, In Memory of Mr. and Mrs. Henry Humphreys, gift of their daughter, Helen: 17 top left. By permission of the Trustees of the British Museum: 17 bottom right, 27 top right, 31 right, 34 top and bottom left, 39 bottom right. The Metropolitan Museum of Art, photograph by Francis G. Mayer: 18 top left, 26. The American Museum of Natural History, photograph by Francis G. Mayer: 20 top right. Photograph by Francis G. Mayer: 21. Bill Vaughn—Black Star: 24 bottom left. Cooper Union Museum, photograph by Francis G. Mayer: 27 bottom right. Hirmer Verlag, Munich: 30 left. Courtesy, Museum of Fine Arts, Boston: 32 top left. Teheran Museum, photograph by Francis G. Mayer: 34 bottom right. Courtesy of Dr. Alfonso Caso: 36 bottom left. Courtesy, Carlo M. Lerici: 40 top centre and right, 41. Professor John P. Bradford: 42 top left; Royal Air Force copyright: 42 bottom left—both courtesy Carlo M. Lerici. National Archaeological Museum, Athens, photograph by Louis H. Frohman: 43.

ARCHAEOLOGY

BY C. W. CERAM

ILLUSTRATED BY PETER SPIER

PAUL HAMLYN · LONDON

Archaeology is numbered among the "conquering sciences of the 19th century". — ADOLF MICHAELIS

THESE BOLD WORDS were written in 1905 by a German archaeologist who was the first historian of archaeological science. ■ Visionary words they were, too. For it was not so clear then as it is now that a science of the past would arise, and by its conquest of what had gone before provide historic balance and serve as a counterweight to the conquest of the future by the physical sciences—thus broadening the whole base of human achievement. *We need the last 5,000 years to bear up with any equanimity under the next 100.* ■ "Archaeology" (Greek *archaiologia,* from *archaios,* ancient, and *logos,* discourse) means "the study of old things". An English encyclopaedia defines it as: "The study of beginnings". ■ At one time this general concept was much narrower. When the word "archaeology" was coined in the 17th century, it denoted "the study of the classic art of antiquity", rediscovered not long before, during the Renaissance. The first collections of antique art had appeared in churches and princely palaces, and the business of arranging and interpreting them had begun. But it was only slowly that archaeology came to be identified with excavation. No one thought to bother about custom, usage, and social structure, the elucidation of which today lends importance to the smallest find. The *art object* was everything; the *object of use,* which to the

Panoramic view of the sculptures and inscriptions on the cliff at Behistun. The inscriptions contained different versions of the same text, which led G. F. Grotefend and H. C. Rawlinson to decipher the Persepolitan cuneiform

modern archaeologist is often more valuable than golden treasure, counted not at all. ■ At the start, too, archaeological activity was confined to Greek or Roman sites. From them archaeology drew its standards. It was blind to all other cultures. This prejudice remained in force until modern times. All young archaeologists went to Athens rather than to Central America, where they could have explored the beginnings of more recent civilizations. (To be sure, educational opportunities for the prospective archaeologist were nowhere better than in Athens and Rome.) ■ Up to the beginning of the 19th century, then, archaeology was preoccupied with the collection of artistic remains, whether found on top of the ground or buried under rubble, ashes, lava, or sand. ■ In this book we shall not follow the Darwinist-evolutionary interpretation of world history as a continuous event (whereby we would have to

Shovel, pick, basket, and tip-truck: these primitive tools, when used by practiced hands, guarantee that nothing will be destroyed. BELOW, the Sphinx, being measured by Napoleon's archaeologists in 1798

include prehistory). We shall limit ourselves for two reasons: first, because we see a marked break between prehistory and the inception, about 4000 B.C., of what became advanced cultures, characterized by organized states, monumental architecture, and written records. Second, because the prehistorian's excavation methods are totally unlike those of the archaeologist working on advanced cultural sites. Laying bare an Ice Age campsite requires a kind of knowledge quite different from that needed in excavating the remains of a Greek temple. And an expert who can undertake to preserve a skeleton need not have the least inkling of how to reconstruct an Early Minoan vase. ■ From the very beginning, "classical" archaeology was faced not only with monuments, but with *inscriptions* as well. Some of these could be read, but many others had to be deciphered. This problem came to have the utmost importance when archaeologists pushed into the East and discovered completely dead and forgotten cultures. ■ As a result, archaeology became a general term covering numerous specialties. The modern Egyptologist knows little about Assyriology, the Assyriologist little about classical archaeology, and the classical archaeologist, in turn, nothing at all about Hittology, or the more recent study of ancient India. He knows even less about American archaeology, which is concerned with the Aztec, Maya, Toltec, Olmec, Zapotec, and Mixtec cultures—not to mention the extraordinary Inca civilization of Peru. ■ The first archaeologists went at old ruins hammer and tongs. Even Schliemann, later to be world-famous, when he was excavating at Troy tore down whole walls if they got in his way. Crowbars, even dynamite, were used in opening up the first pyramids. But today excavation has become a very subtle technique. Pedantically careful teamwork has long since replaced the smash-and-crash approach to graves, temples, and city foundations. Each new dig is carried out under international treaty. These days "robbing graves" is out (except, unhappily, among real grave robbers). Spiriting away the Elgin marbles from Athens would be impossible today. ■ Nevertheless, all restrictions notwithstanding, working in the field is still an adventure—if more an intellectual than a physical one as in pioneer days, when the archaeologist sometimes had to shoot it out with marauding tribesmen. To be eyewitness to the last push of the spade, to see yawn darkly open a grave that had been closed thousands of years before, to unlock the mystery of what the grave contains—the thrill of all this is as great today as it ever was.

Temple of Persepolis reconstruction

Roman Forum, ruins

Roman Forum, reconstruction

Parthenon, reconstruction

Reconstruction—one of archaeology's most controversial problems. Is it permissible at all to reconstruct ruins without knowing exactly how they looked originally? Can ruins really provide indisputable guidelines for a correct reconstruction? The Roman Forum probably once looked like this, since there is a whole literature describing it. But did the Temple of Persepolis and the Parthenon really look as they are shown in reconstruction?

Johann Joachim Winckelmann
(1717–1768)

POMPEII, HERCULANEUM, AND THE "FATHER OF ARCHAEOLOGY"

In 1768 a well-to-do foreigner—his name was Johann Joachim Winckelmann—stopped off at a Trieste hotel during a trip to Italy. That evening an ex-convict came into his room, threw a noose around his neck, and killed and robbed him. ■ Since then almost two centuries have passed. But to this day, on December 9th, archaeological institutes all over the world celebrate this man's birthday as "Winckelmann Day". Born in 1717, the son of a German cobbler in Stendal, he rose to be librarian for the Count of Bünau, near Dresden, and there gave himself up so completely to the art of antiquity that the pursuit shaped the rest of his life. He became a Roman Catholic in order to get a post in Italy. In Rome and Naples he encountered the first really opulent collections of Greek and Roman works of art.

View of Pompeii today

And there he did what no one had done before: he *classified* by style and form, he interpreted artistic content and outlined a picture of antique art which for more than a hundred years (indeed, in part, to this day) determined our image of Hellas. He was able to do this because of the extraordinary richness of the material at his disposal. And few had seen it before him, since it had been only recently amassed. ■ At the Bay of Naples, on August 14, A.D. 79, occurred the catastrophe of which the poet Martial said: "Even gods should not be permitted the likes of this!" Vesuvius erupted and the Roman cities of Herculaneum and Pompeii were destroyed, together with all the people in them. ■ When, seventeen hundred years later, the Renaissance and humanism awakened a taste for antique art, princely connoisseurs began actively looking for ancient art objects. The first excavations at Pompeii were begun in

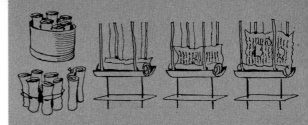

It was Father Piaggi who restored and made legible the almost completely charred rolls of papyrus from the buried cities. Piaggi turned the scorched papyrus a millimeter at a time. Winckelmann, who earlier had been interested only in monuments, thanks to this priest became enthusiastic over documents, which provided him with significant literary disclosures

1826

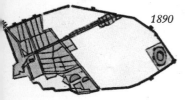

1890

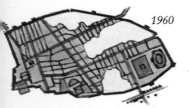

1960

The three plans above show how
Pompeii is being slowly uncovered

The wonderfully heated Roman baths, as in
Pompeii, above, paved the way for the
"bath civilization" of the 20th century

Parboiled eggs, half-done lentils,
nuts, fresh bread—all these were
found in the ruins of Pompeii and
Herculaneum. Some gold coins looked
as though the last paying guest had
just thrown them down

Plaster of Paris corpses. Lava,
rubble, and ashes covered the
bodies of the Pompeians and preserved their outlines as in a mould.
Modern scholars filled up the
moulds and brought the ghostly
drama to life—people in their last
attempt to save a family treasure
or to protect a child

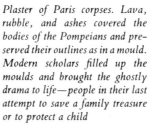

We run into examples of what we consider "modern" civilization on every street of Pompeii. Above, we pass a corner "snack bar"; below, we glance into the courtyard of a rich man's villa

April of 1748, using convict labour. In a few days the first murals were found, then the remains of splendid bronze horses, then statuary. And with them were found an underdone suckling pig in an oven, coins left by a tavern's last paying guests, and skeletons. For the first time the *everyday* look of an ancient city lay revealed to modern eyes. When Goethe viewed the excavations at Pompeii, he wrote: "Many disasters have occurred in the world, but few have given following generations more pleasure. I am hard put to think of anything more interesting". ■ When Winckelmann published, in 1762, his first open letters "On the Discoveries at Herculaneum", then, in 1764, his major work, *History of the Art of Antiquity*, he was able to do so because he had the most priceless material of his day to work with. Material which, to be sure, had been literally "stolen" from the ground —for princely excavators thought of art as treasure. ■ Since then, digs have been carried out again and again, during the last forty years under the supervision of Amadeo Maiuri. But today two-fifths of Pompeii still lies under its 1,900-year-old shroud.

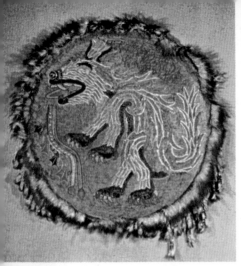

The gift of the Aztec ruler Montezuma to Emperor Charles V of Spain: a shield with feather mosaic representing a prairie wolf. The mosaic, made up of thousands of bird feathers, took years to execute

THE TREASURE HUNTERS Neither scientific nor artistic interest motivated the adventurers who discovered new worlds at the beginning of the 16th century. Treasure was what they sought in Mexico and Peru, and they robbed and murdered to get it. Even so, they also brought home the first reports which, 300 years later, were to provide invaluable data for honest archaeological research. In the Mexico of this period the Aztecs practised human sacrifice. From the year 1519 on, this gave the Christian Spaniard, Hernando Cortes, an excuse to desecrate Aztec temples and ship back their golden treasure to his king. Francisco Pizarro behaved even more shamelessly in Peru. With his 180 men in armour and 33 horses he destroyed the kingdom of the Incas. He had King Atahualpa executed and, like Cortes, sent treasure home —but again, with the treasure, came reports of a high civilization previously unknown to Europeans. ■ Not naked lust for booty, but a covetous desire for artistic treasures, moved Lord Elgin, from 1800 to 1803, to ship the famous Elgin marbles, ornaments from the Parthenon, from Athens to London on the excuse of "preserving them". At first only horse-

LEFT: *Inca gold mask from Mochica, Peru, c. 800 A.D. For the Inca, Maya, and Aztecs, gold was a metal used for ornamentation, not as money. *BELOW: *Aztec skull, 1324–1521 A.D., overlaid with a mosaic of turquoise and obsidian. The eyes are iron pyrites*

breeders saw anything of interest in these animal figures. It was not until more than a decade later that the British Museum bought the treasure for £35,000 so that it might be saved for continuing study. ■ In Egypt men broke into royal graves. Giovanni Belzoni dug up and shipped to London a statue of Ramses—but he left behind drawings of his activities (1820) which a century later had value as source material. And in his day there was already a centuries-old grave-robber tradition among some of the natives. In the village of Kurna near Thebes this was especially true of the family of Abd-el-Rasul, the latest scion of which is today a guard at the same graves his family once plundered. ■ A modern example

Giovanni Belzoni was a fortune-hunter. In 1817 he broke into the tomb of Sethos I. In 1818 he opened the second pyramid of Gizeh, the tomb of King Chephren. When the British Museum commissioned him to ship Egyptian antiquities from Thebes to London, he did not hesitate. Promptly he had a Ramses colossus sent across the seas

of robbery: Statistics compiled during the last 10 years in central Italy, whereby robbed and unrobbed graves were systematically compared, revealed that 80 per cent had been rifled. Some 2,000 ceramic pieces had been stolen from Etruscan graves and smuggled out of the country. In carrying out night grave robberies, 40 to 50 per cent of the finds had been destroyed out of ignorance, adding up to a purely material annual loss to Italy of some 2 billion lire. This means that in the foreseeable future, since in Italy only a thousandth of all antique sites have been excavated, there will be a material loss of more than 100 billion lire over and beyond the irreparable scientific and artistic loss. ■ Today there are strict laws for the protection of antiquities. But no police power in the countries affected is strong enough to stop grave robbery completely, encouraged as it is by greedy dealers.

FIRST TRAVELLERS AND DISCOVERERS Not all archaeological pioneers were treasure hunters. The scientific archaeology of the 19th and 20th centuries can thank the great travellers and discoverers for a wealth of extraordinary material. Many of these men saw, and made drawings of, things which vanished from sight in later decades, destroyed by time or catastrophe. Thus the diary of Johann Helffrich (1579) describes a sphinx then almost intact. In 1569 the missionary Bernardino de Sahagún finished his work on the customs and art of the Aztecs of Mexico. Similarly invaluable are the thousands of letters containing observations made in the classic lands of antiquity during the 17th and 18th centuries by the French travellers Fabri de Peiresc, de Montfaucon, and de Caylus. Earlier a young Roman patrician, Pietro della Valle, having been jilted by his love, went in his grief into the desert—and wandered as far as India. His 3-volume account of his travels (from 1650) is a mine of information. ■ Others sent home from Persepolis (near Shiraz in Iran) the first cuneiform texts, the basis for subsequent ingenious decipherments. The travels of Carsten Niebuhr, who

Persepolis, capital of Persia. Destroyed in 330 B.C.

"Hurry, oh bey! Hurry over here to the workers, for they have found Nimrud himself. O Allah, it is wonderful and true! We have seen him with our own eyes!" Thus shouted his Arab workmen to the English archaeologist Austen Henry Layard as he hastened towards them. In his book Nineveh and Its Remains (1849) he wrote: "They uncovered an enormous human head, chiselled in one piece out of the alabaster of the country ... I saw at once that the head must belong to a winged lion or bull."

The most fabulous discoverer in Central America, next to Humboldt, was certainly the Comte de Waldeck (born 1766), who had himself carried on a litter through the Maya's primeval wilds. En route he wrote, sketched, and was always on the lookout for information out of the past. He had been with Napoleon in Egypt. He first visited Guatemala in 1821 and led an expedition there from 1832–36. He lived to see the Franco-Prussian War and died at 109

reached Arabia in 1762; Abbé Barthélémy's book on Greece, which appeared in 1788; the first excavations in Arabia made by the linguistic genius C. J. Rich in 1811; the fantastic Arabian journeys (from 1809) of J. L. Burckhardt, disguised as "Sheikh Ibrahim"; the jungle ride of John Lloyd Stephens, who, with the artist Frederick Catherwood (from 1839), discovered the Maya culture in Central America; Paul Emile Botta (from 1842) and Austen Henry Layard (from 1845), who breached the Mesopotamian cultures; and dozens of others who travelled amid unutterable dangers—all these people collected material which created the foundation for scientific archaeology.

Frederick Catherwood, Stephens' companion in his conquest of the Maya jungle, was an extraordinarily accurate draftsman. Many of the monuments he saw have been partially destroyed. But his drawings, such as the one at right, show them exactly as they once were, even the hieroglyphs

HEINRICH
SCHLIEMANN

1822 Heinrich Schliemann born in Mecklenburg, Germany, son of a poor minister.

1836 Becomes grocery shop apprentice; works 18 hours a day, for five and a half years.

1841 Cabin boy on a ship; wrecked in North Sea; saved.

1842 Works as clerk in Amsterdam; begins language studies: English, French, Dutch, Spanish, Italian, and Portuguese.

1844 Learns Russian.

1846 Becomes his firm's agent in St. Petersburg.

1850 Banker in California; becomes U.S. citizen; received by President.

1854 Becomes millionaire through indigo trade; learns Swedish and Polish.

1856 Learns modern and ancient Greek; improves his Latin.

1863 After learning Arabic, takes trip round the world.

1866 Now a multi-millionaire, settles in Paris—"in order continuously to devote myself to the study of archaeology."

1868 His book *Ithaca, Archaeological Investigations of Heinrich Schliemann* appears, following the publication of a travel book, *China and Japan*.

1869 Marries 18-year-old Greek girl, Sophia Engastromenos.

1870-73 At his own expense, excavates Troy.

1876 Opens up the five graves in Mycenae, finding the famous "Treasury of Atreus".

1880 At Orchomonos, digs up the "Treasure House of Minyas".

1882 Secures technical assistance of Wilhelm Dörpfeld, co-excavator of Olympia.

1884-85 Digs at Tiryns.

1890 Last dig at Troy; dies the day after Christmas at Naples.

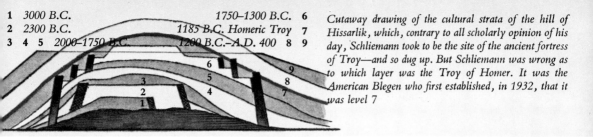

1	3000 B.C.
2	2300 B.C.
3 4 5	2000–1750 B.C.

6	1750–1300 B.C.
7	1185 B.C. Homeric Troy
8 9	1200 B.C.–A.D. 400

Cutaway drawing of the cultural strata of the hill of Hissarlik, which, contrary to all scholarly opinion of his day, Schliemann took to be the site of the ancient fortress of Troy—and so dug up. But Schliemann was wrong as to which layer was the Troy of Homer. It was the American Blegen who first established, in 1932, that it was level 7

ARCHAEOLOGY AS A SCIENCE Archaeology as a truly scientific endeavour did not begin with Heinrich Schliemann. But this dilettante genius who took Homer at his word and, against all expert opinion of his day, actually found Troy and, at Mycenae, the citadel of Atreus and Agamemnon, overnight evoked a worldwide interest in archaeology. ■ Not the least of Schliemann's accomplishments was that he paved the way for a strictly scientific investigation, one that was to become a model of its kind: the excavation, beginning in 1875, of the sacred Greek religious centre at Olympia. For the first time two governments, in this case the German and the Greek, drew up an agreement to regulate the operation. This treaty came to serve as a legal precedent for later digs. Solely in the interest of science a foreign country financed an exploration that lasted for years, meanwhile submitting to supervision by the host country and renouncing claim to anything found except where two or more of a kind were discovered. At Olympia, Ernst Curtius and Wilhelm

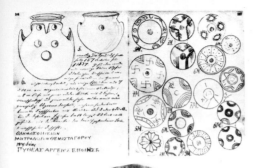

RIGHT: *Sophia Schliemann wearing the "Jewels of Helen". LEFT: a page from Schliemann's diary. BELOW RIGHT: the burial ground Schliemann found when he began digging at Mycenae (from 1876). BELOW LEFT: gold mask found in the Mycenaean graves. Schliemann believed it to be that of Agamemnon*

24

Dörpfeld opened up a thousand years of history. They laid bare the sacred grove and the Temple of Zeus. Yet it is only recently that the Olympic stadium was excavated by E. Kuntze, who earlier had found the workshop of Phidias, creator of one of the Seven Wonders of the Ancient World: the gold and ivory statue of Zeus. There were other archaeological treaties, too. In 1878 Karl Humann began a dig in Asia Minor with the stipulation that two-thirds of all finds should be his. He brought the famous "Altar of Pergamon" to Berlin. In 1900 Sir Arthur Evans began to excavate the multi-storeyed "Palace of Minos" at Knossos in Crete, bringing to light murals never seen before by modern man and discovering unknown scripts—all part of the oldest "European" culture. Steadily he refined his digging methods and reconstructed so boldly that he raised new problems. ■ Precise, hairline measurement had been introduced earlier by Sir Flinders Petrie, who dug for 55 years in Egypt, beginning in 1880. Robert Koldewey resurrected Babylon (from 1898). Leonard Woolley, in subtlest fashion, using whisk, spatula, painter's brush, and his own hands, examined the

Zeus Abducting Ganymede, c. 470 B.C., found at Olympia

royal graves of Ur (from 1922). Howard Carter analyzed the tomb of Tutankhamen (from 1922), after an archaeological find that thrilled the world. C. F. A. Schaeffer laid bare ancient Ugarit (from 1929). Kurt Bittel scientifically reorganized his predecessors' faulty digs at Bogazköy, the Hittite capital in Asia Minor, and by means of new excavations lent contour to an unknown empire. From 1922 on, Sir John Marshall and then R. E. Mortimer Wheeler discovered new riddles in the Indus Valley. A. Parrot, by his find in Mari, in 1933, of 20,000 clay tablets, cast doubt on what had been thought was a reliable dating system. All these archaeological operations represented teamwork rather than individual effort. ■ Today whatever the spade may bring to view is subjected to the excavator's expert judgment. It is localized by architect and surveyor, analyzed by chemist and physicist to determine age and substance, investigated for flora and fauna by botanist and zoologist, stylistically classified by the art historian, and finally smoothed into the broad mosaic of human history by the general historian.

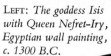

LEFT: *The goddess Isis with Queen Nefret-Iry, Egyptian wall painting, c. 1300 B.C.*

Detail from the Elgin marbles, Parthenon frieze, 447–432 B.C.

Bust of Queen Nefertiti, Egypt, 1375–1357 B.C.

Cylix, Greece, 6th century B.C.

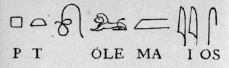

P T   OLE MA   I OS

Egyptian Hieroglyphs

I   S   P   I   S

Persepolitan Cuneiform

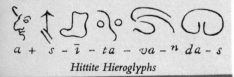

$a + s - \bar{\imath} - ta - va - {}^{n}da - s$

Hittite Hieroglyphs

$$\text{𝕾𝕴𝕵𝕺𝕸𝕵𝕴𝕷𝕸}$$

Undeciphered Easter Island Script

DECIPHERING OF ANCIENT SCRIPTS We have always been able to read Greek and Latin. Thus, Greek and Roman remains have lived and their inscriptions have spoken to us. But the monuments of the East for long said not a word. ■ In 1802, at 27, and merely to win a bet, the German teacher Georg F. Grotefend succeeded within a few weeks in deciphering cuneiform writing. This feat went unnoticed until independently repeated in 1846 by a young Englishman, Henry C. Rawlinson. After 15 years of preparation, the Frenchman Jean-François Champollion in 1822 published his decipherments of the Egyptian hieroglyphs. The task of decoding the Cretan script took over 50 years, but it was finally accomplished in 1953 by an English amateur, Michael Ventris. In 1945 Helmuth T. Bossert found a bilingual inscription in Anatolia—and Hittite hieroglyphs finally became intelligible. In 1962 two Russian scholars announced an apparently valid decipherment of Maya hieroglyphs. ■ But countless ancient forms of writing still cannot be clearly read. They include Etruscan, the Easter Island, the Indus Valley, the Carian, the Sinai, and many others.

WONDER ON THE NILE Egyptian archaeology began with Napoleon's conquest of Egypt. Results were collected in a monumental work and published from 1809 onward. The German Karl Richard Lepsius, from 1842, took up the torch and pushed the bounds of Egyptian history back into the fourth millennium B.C. The Frenchman Auguste Marriette unearthed a whole series of temples, put a stop to grave robbery, and founded the Egyptian Museum. Countless archaeologists worked at clarifying the problems of pyramid building and sorting out styles and periods. Meanwhile the historians began to chronicle the story of ancient Egypt in greater detail than had the ancient Greeks and Romans. ■ Today Egypt faces a singular problem: the greatest earth dam in the world is being built at Aswan, a structure that will save hundreds of thousands of Egyptians from hunger. But the backed-up

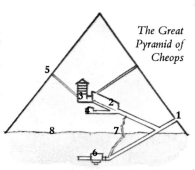

The Great Pyramid of Cheops

1 *Entrance*
2 *Great Hall*
3 *King's chamber*
4 *Queen's chamber*
5 *Airshafts*
6 *Subterranean chamber*
7 *Connecting shaft*
8 *Bedrock*

Napoleon's scientists inspecting the Great Hall of the Pyramid

waters of the dam will inundate hundreds of ancient Egyptian monuments, among them the Ramses Temple at Abu Simbel. This prospect has pricked the conscience of the world. Money is pouring into UNESCO, and since 1961 a grandiose technical scheme has been introduced to save the oldest remains of human history.

The gold portrait mask of Pharaoh Tutankhamen (c. 1350 B.C.) and the burial chamber of his pyramid, as it appeared when first opened.

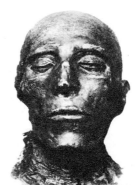

*The Egyptians believed that the body had to be preserved for its
ka (spirit, soul). The corpse (as above) was eviscerated, salted
for a month, dried for 70 days, wrapped endlessly in bandages
soaked in a resinous material, and then placed in its coffin.
Eventually the Egyptians learned how to wrap without using
string or glue (detail above). Mummification was for long a
mystery. Today we know that its success depended on almost
bacteria-free air and soil.* RIGHT: *the mummified head of King
Sethos, after unwrapping.* FAR RIGHT: *a coffin with portrait
mask, paintings, and cuneiform writing*

Lion on the Sacred Way, the processional street leading from the Ishtar Gate to the temple of Marduk

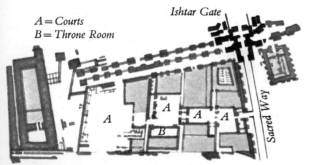

A = Courts
B = Throne Room

Ishtar Gate

Sacred Way

LEFT: *Plan of the palaces of Babylon. They were approached from the Sacred Way, through the Ishtar Gate, main entrance to the city. The Gate and palaces date from the 6th cent. B.C.* ABOVE: *The first column of the Gate to appear during the earliest excavations. The archaeologist Koldewey had no idea of the gigantic dimensions of the Gate; in some places he had to dig 75 feet to uncover it completely.* ABOVE RIGHT: *Babylon after the excavations. Koldewey worked 19 years to unearth the magnificent ruins that had been buried and forgotten for two and a half millennia.* BELOW RIGHT: *Koldewey's reconstruction of the Ishtar Gate*

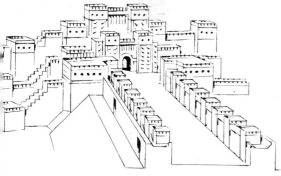

IN BIBLE LANDS Although no Christian had ever had the right to doubt the word of the Scriptures, it was still a great source of amazement when, from the 18th century on, innumerable Old Testament sites mentioned in the Bible were actually brought to light after thousands of years of only hearsay existence. Beginning in 1842, the Frenchman Paul Emile Botta and the Englishman Austen Henry Layard excavated Nineveh. Several nations contributed to the excavation of Babylon, with the German Robert Koldewey, beginning in 1899, carrying the work through to completion. From 1888 to 1900 Americans entered the international picture for the first time when John Peters and Hermann Hilprecht dug up Nippur and Fara. Ever deeper into the past struck the archaeologist's spade. Ur, home of Abraham, was opened up. The hitherto unknown Sumerian culture was discovered. The

land between the Tigris and the Euphrates seemed to be the cradle of mankind. A few years ago city foundations more than 6,000 years old were found at Jericho. ■ Proof that exciting finds are still possible even today is evidenced in the discovery, by a goatherd in 1947, of the first seven Scriptural scrolls in a cave on the Dead Sea, the oldest texts we have on the origins of Christianity.

LEFT: King Assurbanipal Hunting Lions, *relief from the Palace at Nineveh, 668–630 B.C.*

BELOW LEFT: The *"Standard of Ur"*, side representing *"Peace". First half, 3rd millennium B.C.* RIGHT: *portrait of a prince, possibly Xerxes, Persepolis, 5th century B.C.*

THE "NEW" WORLD, WHICH PROVED TO BE OLD The conquests of the Spanish conquistadors in Central and South America had always been of interest to historians, but only as political events. Not until the 19th century was it realized that these wild soldiers had discovered highly organized cultures. ■ Viscount Kingsborough died of typhus in 1831 in a Dublin debtors' prison. But before he died he had published a work in 7 volumes showing the first big collection of Mexican antiquities. He ruined himself financially to obtain his now priceless collection. ■ A sensation was created when the American John L. Stephens, with his illustrator Frederick Catherwood, brought out (from 1842) his reports on the Maya temples and sculptures—for world archaeological interest was then fixed on Greek and Roman antiquities. But even in 1912, when Hiram Bingham discovered the Inca citadel of

*Machu Picchu, Inca citadel
2,000 feet above Urubamba River*

The eight-tiered pyramid at Palenque, with the "Temple of Inscriptions" at top. Here, in a 14-by-30-foot burial chamber, Alberto Ruz found the skeleton of a Maya ruler. The greatest horde of old Mexican treasure was found in 1931 in the temple mound of Monte Alban at Oaxaca. The gold mask below was found there

1 Entrance
2 Staircase (45 steps)
3 Landing
4 Staircase (21 steps)
5 Sarcophagus
6 Burial Chamber

Machu Picchu, historians scarcely knew what to make of it. Generations of archaeologists were needed to give Central and South American civilizations their rightful niche in cultural history. ■ Today the cultures of the Maya (from about A.D. 200 to their destruction by the Spaniards), of the Aztecs (from A.D. 1300 to their destruction), and above all of the Incas (from A.D. 1200) are the subject of a most intensive investigation. The point of critical interest is whether these highly organized civilizations grew up independently or as offshoots of the classic Oriental-Chinese culture. This problem has not yet been solved.

KINGDOM OF THE HITTITES One of the most astonishing discoveries of 20th-century archaeology was the Hittite empire of Asia Minor. This civilization had already conquered Babylon by 1600 B.C., and in 1296 B.C., at Kadesh, annihilated the Egyptian Ramses, greatest ruler of the ancient world. These Hittite people, it was found, developed an advanced literature, worked out the basic technique of "modern" horse breeding, and invented the light war chariot. ■ The French traveller Charles Texier (from 1833) brought back the first reports of nameless ruins in Anatolia. After the Czech Friedrich Hrozny (from 1915) had deciphered the Hittite cuneiform, dead stones began to speak. French, American, and, later, Turkish archaeologists dug up city after city. The German Kurt Bittel is now in his third decade of excavation at the Hittite capital of Hattushash, near present-day Bogazköy.

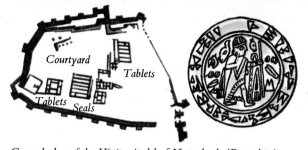

Ground plan of the Hittite citadel of Hattushash (Bogazköy), where thousands of tablets and seals are still being found. The "Tarkumuwa Seal" shows Hittite hieroglyphs and cuneiforms, a combination which made it possible to decipher the former.
BELOW: *North Gate of Karatepe, Hittite seat of petty kings*

ABOVE: *Stepped entrance at Shishupalarh in India.* BELOW LEFT: *An Indian seal with an as-yet undeciphered script.* BELOW RIGHT: *A terra-cotta sarcophagus from the city of Pellavaram*

INDUS VALLEY CIVILIZATION In 1856 the brothers J. and W. Brunton undertook to build the first railway through the Indus Valley. They were told of old ruins in the jungle and used gigantic city foundations 5,000 years old as a source of stone to provide ballast for their roadbed. ■ First to recognize the value of this find was General Alexander Cunningham, who found the first seal with written characters among the rubble. Some 66 years later it was an Indian, R. D. Banerji, who realized that Mohenjo-Daro and Harappa had once been great centres of civilization—well-planned cities with excellent water systems supplying hot and cold water, original art forms, and their own method of writing. Later, from 1922, Sir John Marshall, collaborating with Indian archaeologist N. G. Majumdar, undertook extensive excavations. The task was carried forward, from 1945, by Dr. R. E. M. Wheeler. Today a vast amount of material from this ancient civilization has been made available. But we still do not know the relation of the Indus Valley to the equally ancient Mesopotamian civilizations. Nor are we able to read the script, one of the oldest known to mankind.

MODERN METHODS This book could well be called *From Grave Robbery to Scientific Archaeology*. We first saw archaeology as a "scientific" enterprise in the Olympia dig. Yet even so, how often since then have sins been committed, through lack of understanding, bad organization, or overzealous dilettantism. ■ Archaeological research received a completely new impetus after World War II. Methods developed in the physical sciences and nuclear physics proved to be astonishingly helpful. Examples of this are atmospheric analysis, originally used for military purposes; boring for oil and water by modern geophysically determined means; underwater exploration; and the like. ■ Credit for the most significant discovery must go to the American W. F. Libby. His is the "radiocarbon dating" method, a physical means whereby the age of organic material, whether 1,000 or 5,000 years old, can

Sculpture from an Etruscan sarcophagus, 6th–5th centuries B.C. It is of painted terra cotta. The sculpture shown in black and white is from a fake sarcophagus and dates only from 1860

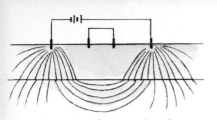

Diagram showing Lerici's new method of using electricity to explore subterranean hollow spaces, especially graves. The cutaway drawing below shows a grave being examined, while closed, by means of Lerici's inverted periscope

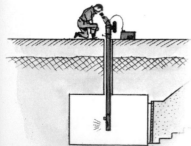

be precisely measured, and with it the age of the site where the material is found. By this method the age of organic matter found in the tombs of the Pharaohs suddenly became *measurable!* ■ Knowing that even now a ship goes down every day somewhere in the seven seas, it is not at all remarkable that countless ships carrying art treasures to Rome from Greece and the East should have foundered in the past on the Mediterranean coast. As early as 1900 deep-sea divers began to bring up the first treasure from this "Blue Museum". But not until the skin diver came along, equipped with Capt. J. Y. Cousteau's aqualung, was it possible to make treasure dives to antique vessels with certain prospect of success. ■ Aerial photography, already under development in World War I, after

By using modern methods for archaeological excavation, Carlo Lerici has added enormously to our knowledge of the Etruscans. When a grave has been located and the hole dug for the periscope, it can be determined if the grave is worth opening up. The pictures at left and below show part of what was seen in one grave, which was subsequently opened: the superb paintings from the "Tomb of the Olympiads"

World War II was put to systematic use by archaeologists. An aerial photograph can reveal vegetation and contour differences on the surface of the earth that provide clear clues to ancient burial grounds. ■ An engineer and industrialist who was an expert in boring for oil and water—the Italian Carlo Lerici—in 1955 took up archaeology as a hobby. He put to use geophysical methods in sounding out Etruscan graves, particularly in the neighbourhood of modern Tarquinia, not far from Rome. In one season's work, with the aid of these methods, he discovered many hundreds of graves—

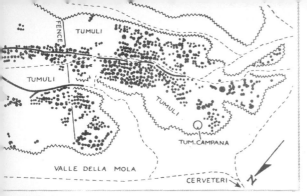

ABOVE: *underwater archaeology, at the site of an ancient shipwreck. An elaborate system of mapping frames, bedspring-like grids, and surveying poles makes it possible for the diver-archaeologist to plot the position of artifacts, in this case, globe-shaped amphorae. Much of the surveying is done with underwater cameras.* LEFT: *The original aerial photograph of an Etruscan burying ground, made recognizable by differences in vegetation not noticeable from the ground. Above it is the graphic evaluation made from the photograph and used as a basis for investigation. It was the French priest, Father A. Poidebard, who first successfully used aerial photography in archaeology.* FAR RIGHT: *Bronze statue of Poseidon found in the sea off Cape Artemision, Greece, in 1929*

more than archaeologists using conventional means had found in the last 200 years. He also invented the "inverted periscope", a tube with lenses that can be thrust into a grave. With this device he could photograph the contents of a grave and tell beforehand whether full-scale excavation was worth the bother. ■ Means of detecting archaeological frauds have been particularly refined in the past few decades. At first it was the X ray that helped; today it is a whole variety of techniques drawn from physics, chemistry, biology, carbon dating, and so on. ■ Every day sees an enrichment of our knowledge of ancient cultures, of the streams that since 5,000 years ago, by endless roundabout ways, have been flowing into our own culture. We are now able to feed on the experience of countless generations. Will the archaeologists help us to *learn* from this experience? That is not their task—but ours!

MILESTONES IN ARCHAEOLOGY

1506, Laocoön group discovered at Rome with Michelangelo looking on. **1666,** Royal Society in London promotes investigation of ruins of Persepolis. **1711,** first statues found in Herculaneum. **1748,** excavation of Pompeii begins. **1753,** scrolls found in "Villa dei Papiri" in Herculaneum. **1764,** Winckelmann publishes *History of the Art of Antiquity*. **1787,** del Rio undertakes first investigation of Mexican ruins. **1798,** Napoleon goes to Egypt. His Scientific Commission lays groundwork for modern Egyptology. **1799,** trilingual Rosetta Stone found on Nile, making possible decipherment of hieroglyphs. **1800,** Lord Elgin begins to ship most important parts of Parthenon frieze to England. **1802,** G. F. Grotefend deciphers cuneiform. **1811,** C. J. Rich makes his first digs in Babylon. **About 1820,** "Venus de Milo" found by peasant at Melos. **1822,** J. F. Champollion deciphers Egyptian hieroglyphs. **1827,** first Etruscan murals found in graves at Tarquinia, northwest of Rome. **1830,** K. O. Müller's *Handbook of Archaeology* appears. **1833,** C. Texier begins investigation of Asia Minor and is first to describe Hittite capital of Hattushash. **1842,** J. L. Stephens publishes his discoveries in Central American kingdom of the Maya. **1842,** P. E. Botta begins excavations in Assyria. **1842,** Lepsius discovers first of more than 60 pyramids in Egypt. **1845,** A. H. Layard begins excavation of Nineveh. **1858,** at Knidos, Newton for first time lays bare the ground plan of an antique city. **1865,** K. Humann arrives for first time at Pergamon. **1868,** H. Schliemann makes his first trip to Troy. **1875,** digs under E. Curtius at Olympia begin. **1878,** M. Kalokairinos uncovers labyrinth at Knossos on Crete. **1880,** W. Flinders Petrie begins 55 years of investigation in Egypt. **1887,** clay tablet archives of Tell-el-Amarna found by chance. **1887,** E. Seler begins laying foundation of modern American archaeology in Mexico. **1888,** American digs at Nippur begin under Peters. **1893,** T. Homolle begins excavations at Delphi. **1898,** R. Koldewey begins 18-year excavation of Babylon. **1899,** Baalbek expedition begins under O. Puchstein. **1900,** A. Evans begins 25-year excavation of Knossos. **1900,** divers find sunken Roman ship in Mediterranean. **1903,** W. Andrae begins to open up Assur. **1906,** H. Winckler and T. Macridi-Bey find first library of clay tablets at Hattushash, Hittite capital. **1911,** A. Maiuri initiates modern excavation of Pompeii. **1912,** H. Bingham discovers old Inca fortress of Machu Picchu. **1915,** F. Hrozny deciphers Hittite cuneiform. **1922,** L. Woolley begins excavating Royal Cemetery at Ur. **1922,** H. Carter finds tomb of Tutankhamen. **1929,** C. F. A. Schaeffer begins dig at Ugarit. **1931,** K. Bittel and R. Naumann begin excavation of Hittite Hattushash. **1933,** A. Parrot begins dig at Mari and finds clay tablet archives. **1947,** F. Steele puts together oldest lawbook in world out of cuneiform fragments. **1947,** Dead Sea Scrolls found. **1952,** W. F. Libby develops radiocarbon dating method. **1953,** M. Ventris deciphers Cretan script. **1954,** Z. Goneim discovers a step-pyramid at Sakkara and Z. Nour a "Ship of the Dead" in Pyramid of Cheops. **1962,** Russian scholars announce they have deciphered the Maya hieroglyphs. **1963,** priest's tomb discovered in Maya pyramid at Tikal.

INDEX

Temple of the Holy Tooth, Ceylon

Aqueduct of Hadrian, North Africa, c. A.D. 97

Early Minoan vessel, 2500–2000 B.C.

Colossus of Memnon, Thebes, Egypt, 1500 B.C.

Comb, Egypt, New Kingdom

Drinking horn, Iran, 500 B.C.

Tomb of the daughter of Antony and Cleopatra, Algeria

Temple of Hagiar Kim, Malta, 2500 B.C.

Trajan's column, Rome, A.D. 114

Temple of Ellora, India, A.D. 8th cent.